ideals
VALENTINE

Caught in a climate
So callous and cold,
Born of a bearing
Benumbing and bold,
There is a pause
That defies winter's way
Known unto people
As Valentine's Day.

Not in the summer
When weather is warm,
Not in the season
That's senseless to storm,
Not when the birds and
The blooms are their best—
No, it arrives when the
Days are distressed.

This is symbolic—
A heart where it shows,
Melting for others
Their mantle of snows,
Giving life's ribs
An affectionate shove;
Such is the soul
And the substance of love.

Margaret Rorke

ISBN 0-8249-1008-7 350

IDEALS—Vol. 39, No. 1 January MCMLXXXII IDEALS (ISSN 0019-137X) is published eight times a year,
January, February, April, June, July, September, October, November
by IDEALS PUBLISHING CORPORATION, 11315 Watertown Plank Road, Milwaukee, Wis. 53226
Second class postage paid at Milwaukee, Wisconsin. Copyright © MCMLXXXI by IDEALS PUBLISHING CORPORATION.
POSTMASTER: Send address changes to Ideals, Post Office Box 2100, Milwaukee, Wis. 53201
All rights reserved. Title IDEALS registered U.S. Patent Office.
Published simultaneously in Canada.

ONE YEAR SUBSCRIPTION—eight consecutive issues as published—$15.95
TWO YEAR SUBSCRIPTION—sixteen consecutive issues as published—$27.95
SINGLE ISSUE—$3.50

Publisher, James A. Kuse
Managing Editor, Ralph Luedtke
Editor/Ideals, Colleen Callahan Gonring
Associate Editor, Linda Robinson
Production Manager, Mark Brunner
Photographic Editor, Gerald Koser
Copy Editor, Barbara Nevid
Art Editor, Duane Weaver

Barberry Red

O Barberry, red Barberry, smiling in the snow,
When all the fragile summer blooms
Are dreams of long ago,
The frosty rime is on your leaf
And winter's sting o'erhead;
But courage red is ripening
Your berries' gleam of red.

The pond is frozen silver clear;
The sundial's mounded high
With drifted snow-stars glistening
Beneath a leaden sky.
The little snowbirds chirrup
In your sheltering cheery halls;
O Barberry red, you light new faith
When shrouded winter falls.

Anne M. Robinson

Looking for Spring

In February when few gusty flakes
Above the frozen sheets of snow still hover,
Out of his hole the sleepy groundhog breaks
To peek around to see if winter's over.

Now if he finds his shadow, back he shies
To nap while deeper drifts the wind shall bring;
But if no shadow shows beneath dark skies,
He waddles through the ditch to look for spring.

Marnie Pomeroy

Winter Valentines

February is
  the month
Of frosty pines,
Silver etchings
  on windowpanes,
And valentines.

February means
  snowflakes
Lazily drifting down
That add a lacy edge
To the balsam's gown.

The month of February
Is a blessing indeed,
With beauty
  on every hand
To meet each
  heart's need.

Earle J. Grant

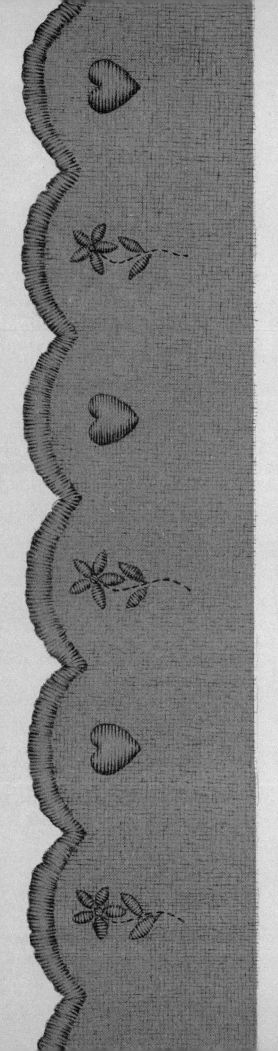

What Is Love?

Carl Goeller

Love is that wonderful, intangible something which has inspired painters, poets, philosophers, preachers, and, most of all, men and women since time began.

To the painter, love is the eyes of a mother as she gazes at her sleeping child ... the embrace of two lovers ... a small boy holding tightly to his father's hand ... and a sunrise on a dew-drenched morning.

The poet sees love as the first breeze of spring ... the blushing glance between a boy and a girl ... the handclasp between friends which says, "I understand you" ... and a special magic which renders all things beautiful.

The philosopher will tell you that love is an unforgettable meeting of two souls ... an invisible bond between man and woman, youth and age ... that feeling which causes one human being to weep unashamedly as he tells another, "I'm sorry."

To the preacher, love is that gift from God which makes Him God ... which allows man his first glimpse of heaven ... and offers him a way to reach it.

Love is magic. It can be all of these, or none of them, because it is completely new every time it happens. It can be found anywhere ... anytime ... anyplace ... by anyone ... and once it is found, nothing is ever quite the same.

Because of You

Because of you my heart is glad today,
And through my mind there runs a soft refrain
Of song, that echoes as I work or play,
Because I soon shall hear your voice again.
The sun is brighter than it was before
Because I know your love is ever true.
The sky is bluer through the open door,
And I am well content because of you.

Now, ever in my heart, there seems to be
An aim, an ardent wish, a constant prayer
That any place my duty beckons me,
That you'll be ever faithful, near me there;
That through the mist of swiftly passing years,
Your love will still remain so tried and true;
That I can wait and laugh at all my fears
And whisper, "I'm content," because of you.

Eunice Elmore Heizer

The Weather's Frightful?
Make the Fun Delightful!

Bea Bourgeois

Believe it or not, keeping children entertained indoors during a frigid snap of winter weather can be wonderful fun. After wrestling with icy zippers on a pair of wet boots or hanging up the last of the drenched mittens, parents could use a little indoor diversion themselves. There are hundreds of entertaining alternatives that will easily lure children away from the monotony of television.

So first, turn off the TV. Decide which activity you and your children will most enjoy.

Go to the shelf—in the attic, or the closet, or the front hall—where you've stored all the jigsaw puzzles. There's nothing nicer than gathering around a card table, everyone trying to find "that ziggedy piece with part of the dog's nose on it." Puzzles feature an extra added attraction: they tend to be extremely calming occupations, and the little ones get so engrossed they even forget to wiggle.

After an hour or so, when your eyes are getting tired and the young ones are convinced that one piece is missing, take a hot chocolate break. Let the kids plop marshmallows on top of theirs, or stir in some gooey marshmallow creme for a sweet, warm treat.

Take an hour out of your winter day and play one of the hundreds of board games that have kept people entertained for years. You, too, can become a wealthy landlord by putting up houses and hotels on Boardwalk and Park Place. Then sit back to watch innocent victims land on your high-class properties. Good old Monopoly® also teaches youngsters a few basic facts about money, and often it's very much like the real world: easy come, easy go. Let's hope they don't have to mortgage all four railroads to pay the rent!

What about all those photo albums you've been meaning to bring up-to-date? Find all the fat envelopes of snapshots that were developed after last summer's vacation, and enlist the help of your children to put them into albums. Some wonderful reminiscences can take place while you're laughing at the size of the perch someone caught or talking about how much you miss those favorite aunts and uncles.

That project might even inspire a child (with a little encouragement from mom and dad) to write a letter or to design some homemade valentines. Help with the spelling of those big, difficult words if you have to. Everyone loves to get mail, especially a thoughtful greeting. The receiver will be delighted, and the sender gets an impromptu lesson in remembering others.

Inexpensive Bingo games are available everywhere, and inside the box are endless hours of silly family fun. To spice up the competition and make the game really worth winning, take a few minutes before you start to play. Find some small treasures around the house—that key chain you got from the bank, the ball-point pen from your insurance agent, or even a few loose nickels—and put them in brown paper lunch sacks. Winners of each round get to pick a prize bag, and there might even be some negotiating to switch prizes after it's all over.

Children love to help in the kitchen, and this is a great opportunity for a beginning baking lesson. Choose a simple recipe, preferably one that produces something scrumptious. A batch of fudge or brownies, some easy bar cookies, or those perennially favorite chocolate chips would be both easy and fun for youngsters. Kids love to mix the dough—don't be surprised if they favor their own two hands over a wooden spoon, and they're always impressed with the end product. If you're planning a dinner they can help with, so much the better. Peeling potatoes is an art quickly learned by small hands, and there's even something satisfying about tearing up hunks of lettuce for a salad. Who knows? You may spark the interest of a future graduate of the Cordon Bleu!

Winter is a perfect time for children to start a scrapbook. Gather up all the outdated magazines that are cluttering up the house, provide a pair of scissors and some school glue or rubber cement, and let their imaginations take over. Some little folks might decide to concentrate on pictures of animals; others might want to collect all the pictures of cars they can find; others might decide to paste in all the cartoons that tickle their funny bones. Older children might want to plan their dream home by snipping out interior designs that appeal to them. Whatever the choice, a scrapbook is a lot of fun to make—and even more fun to look through years later.

Anyone who has a talent for sewing can pass on hours of entertainment to winter-weary children. How about getting a head start on next year's Christmas ornaments? A few scraps of felt, some beads or glitter, an assortment of odd-looking buttons can be trans-

formed into a handmade decoration that will hold a store of memories in years to come.

If the children are old enough, have a few rounds of the Dictionary Game. One player is chosen as the director; he or she chooses any word from the dictionary and writes down its proper definition. All the other players have to define the word, writing their definition as it would appear in a real dictionary. The game is even funnier if the players have to make up definitions, incidentally. When all definitions have been written, the director reads them all, and the players vote on the definition they think is the correct one. The player whose answer receives the most votes is the winner of that round. You'd be surprised what some people think "pavid" means! Subliminally and painlessly, the kids also increase their vocabularies while they're playing the game.

Use the simple things you have around the house to provide a change of pace during playtime. A shoe box turned upside down with the end flaps cut off makes a wonderful tunnel for small cars and trucks to run through. A few wooden clothespins can become a round-headed doll family; kids can draw eyes, noses, mouths, and hair for all the family members, and the dolls can be dressed in a variety of fabric scraps that would never be used. A deck of cards can become a test of patience and skill as youngsters see who can build the tallest house of cards before it collapses to the floor.

There's an old saying that "in the spring, the rivers and the children run wild." So enjoy the frosty, quiet times of winter; before you know it, the children will be bounding out the door into the sunshine, "running wild."

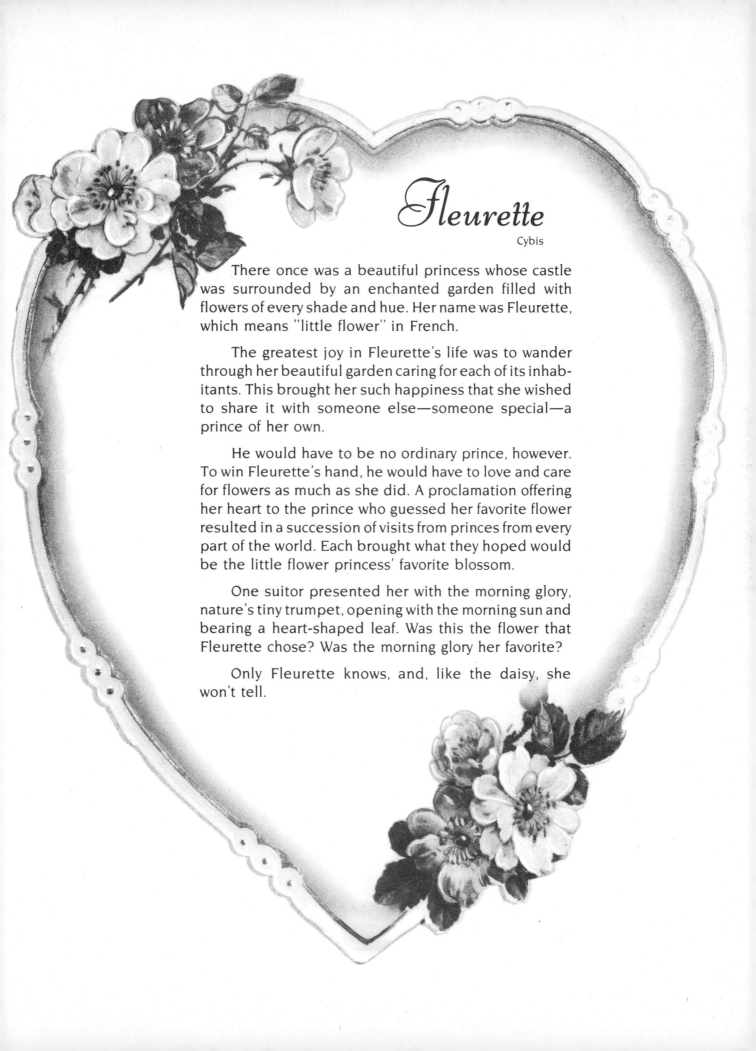

Fleurette

Cybis

There once was a beautiful princess whose castle was surrounded by an enchanted garden filled with flowers of every shade and hue. Her name was Fleurette, which means "little flower" in French.

The greatest joy in Fleurette's life was to wander through her beautiful garden caring for each of its inhabitants. This brought her such happiness that she wished to share it with someone else—someone special—a prince of her own.

He would have to be no ordinary prince, however. To win Fleurette's hand, he would have to love and care for flowers as much as she did. A proclamation offering her heart to the prince who guessed her favorite flower resulted in a succession of visits from princes from every part of the world. Each brought what they hoped would be the little flower princess' favorite blossom.

One suitor presented her with the morning glory, nature's tiny trumpet, opening with the morning sun and bearing a heart-shaped leaf. Was this the flower that Fleurette chose? Was the morning glory her favorite?

Only Fleurette knows, and, like the daisy, she won't tell.

St. Valentine's Day

Lucky for us that Valentine
Went courting with his pen,
Thus to midwinter cold and bleak
A springtime beauty lend.

Blossoming forth in lovely flowers,
In candies ribbon-tied,
In valentines, whose every verse
Are cupid's side by side,

Laughing at stern realities,
A world will stop to play;
Old hearts grow young; young hearts age
On this St. Valentine's Day.

Essie L. Mariner

A Child's Gift

A child who bears a gift of love,
Whatever it may bring,
Will give entirely of its heart—
A great and precious thing.

A gift that's brought with silent grin,
Half fearful as shy birds,
Expresses love with eloquence,
Without the need for words.

Roy Z. Kemp

Dear Old Golden Rule Days

Away back when Johnny and Joanie could read, they could write also. Furthermore, they did write— often on the flyleaves of their textbooks and, as they grew older, in "Memory Books."

This was going on at least as long ago as great-great-grandmother's school days. In that era of slates and quill pens, one particular student wrote in the front of one of his texts:

Abraham Lincoln is my name,
And with my pen I wrote the same.
I wrote it in both haste and speed
And left it here for you to read.

Like Abe, some weren't content merely to sign their names as proof of book ownership. You may have seen or, in your own school days, used this little gem:

If this book should cease to roam,
Give it a kick and send it home
to—Johnny Smith.

Some used those temptingly blank white leaves to wax lyrical about crawling things and creatures with wings. The owner of one history book in 1911 inscribed its front flyleaf with:

See the spider on the wall?
He ain't got no clothes at all;
He ain't got no chemi-shirt;
He ain't got no pettiskirt.
Bo-o-oh! Ain't he cold?

By 1920, that had evolved to:

Little fly upon the wall,
Ain't you got no clothes at all?
Ain't you got no shimmy shirt?
Ain't you got no pettiskirt?
Woo-o-o! Ain't you cold?

Some of the older girls got a little mushy in a modest sort of way. This one was penned about 1904.

Roses were made to blossom;
Cheeks were made to blush;
Arms were made to rest in;
Lips were made to ... Oh, hush!

Once in a while some impish budding genius would become vocal in the classroom. Wasn't there at least one character in your classes who improvised, plagiarized, or revised in some way in order to annoy the teacher? One of my classmates was a puckish lad whose name, I'll say, was Abbot. Part of our assignment for one day was to memorize a verse of some classical American poet's work. Abbot chose the opening one from John Greenleaf Whittier's "The Barefoot Boy."

Whittier, in case you don't remember, started it with:

Blessings on thee, little man,
Barefoot boy with cheek of tan!

Abbot recited:

Blessings on thee, little feller,
Barefoot kid with cheeks of yeller!

before Miss Norwood banished him to the cloakroom.

Not all the verbal versions were even that high-class. If a comrade inadvertently used two words that rhymed with each other in a conversational sentence, someone was sure to interrupt raucously with:

Hey! You're a poet
Same as a sheep is a go-et.

When the great day came on which classes let out for summer vacation, the "poetry" continued. Running backwards with their faces toward the schoolhouse, hoping to see the teacher looking out a window, the bolder erstwhile pupils chanted at full-lung capacity:

Good-bye school days! Good-bye school!
Good-bye teacher and golden rule!

One of the boys wondered if God had punished him for this. As he finished the chant, he whirled about to leave the schoolyard and ran violently and painfully, face first, into a tree to the hysterical, hilarious, falling-down-and-rolling-on-the-ground delight of his pals who saw it.

Ultimately when graduation days came, whether from grammar school or high school, the "Memory Books" came out. Few schools were affluent enough in those days to have yearbooks in which to collect farewell verses and autographs. Consequently, the girls had little notebooks with blank pages in which friends were asked to write something memorable.

One entry, common as far back as 1881, went:

> Forget me not;
> Forget me never
> Until the sun
> Has set forever.
>
>> Your best friend always,
>>> Joanie Doe

Now, dedicated to those who have read this far, here is a spritely gem from 1882:

> I wish thee health;
> I wish thee wealth;
> I wish thee gold a store;
> I wish thee Heaven after death—
> What could I wish thee more?

William J. Denson

A Day of Sweetness

A day of love—a
Day of sweetness
Where candy hearts
Are made just for
You and me—
And if you want,
You may share my
Heart. You see
It is full of
Sweetness and soft
Colors of the rainbow.
So come, come share
My candy heart
And the sweetness
Found within this
Fourteenth day of
February.

W. R. Morrison

A Day of Love

St. Valentine! A special day
   For lovers, tried and true;
Its customs are so very old,
   And yet they're ever new.
So it's no matter if you send
   A paper valentine
With ribbons, lace, and lettering,
   A sentimental line;
Some flowers, or candy, or a gift—
   Perhaps a jewel rare—
To fan the flame of sentiment
   In heart of lady fair.
St. Valentine will still approve
   If given in his name,
No matter what the price or style,
   For love is just the same.

Letitia Morse Nash

Love Stories of America's Castles

Walter Oleksy

Lyndhurst Castle
Tarrytown on Hudson, New York
Photograph by Tom Donia

If love as well as faith can move mountains, it can also build castles.

Across America in almost every state, there is at least one castle which can rival the most splendid to be found anywhere in the world.

The castles were built in America by millionaires, many of whom came to this country as penniless immigrants. After becoming wealthy from railroads, oil, banking, or other pursuits, they fulfilled boyhood dreams of owning a castle and living like a king.

And that is where the love stories come in. Many of the castles were built in order to win the heart of a fair young American maiden by promising her the castle to live in like a queen. The offer proved irresistible for more than a dozen young women, and they soon lived the life of royalty in Gothic, Medieval, Norman, or Eastern-style castles on magnificently landscaped grounds, amid furnishings worth several kings' ransoms.

Samuel T. Soult, a famous architect around the turn of the century, was in the autumn of his years when he fell in love with a beautiful girl of seventeen. He overheard her say she would love to live in a castle, so he offered to build her one if she would marry him. He built a fortress simply called The Castle on a hill overlooking Berkeley Springs, West Virginia.

In the Blue Ridge Mountains of Virginia just west of Charlottesville, Major James Dooley, a Confederate veteran from Richmond, spent more than a million dollars to construct a castle for his bride.

"Build for my Sallie May majestic terraced gardens . . . and a long, marble-columned pergola overlooking the valleys below," Dooley instructed the architect. The white marble castle, built high in the mountains, was named Swannanoa after Indians who once roamed Virginia.

A Moorish castle was built on a hill just across the Hudson River from West Point in New York state by millionaire Evans R. Dick to please his bride. On their honeymoon in Spain, she had become so entranced by the Alhambra that Dick built a replica of it for her back home.

In the North Dakota Badlands, a wealthy Frenchman, the Marquis de Mores, built a castle called Chateau de Mores in 1883 as a wedding present for a red-haired beauty, Medora Hoffman. Not only did he build her the castle, he built her an entire town around his meat-packing business.

George W. Vanderbilt spent some of his millions having one of America's most elaborate castles built in Asheville, North Carolina. It began in 1890 as a summer home and showplace for his growing collection of artwork and antiques. A bachelor of twenty-two when the castle, called Biltmore House, was begun, Vanderbilt gave it to his bride as a wedding present when it was completed five years later.

John Hays Hammond, inventor and organ manufacturer, also had his castle, Hammond Castle, built between 1925 and 1928 for his bride. It recreates court life in Europe during the sixteenth century but also mixes cultures and periods. The Great Hall opens onto a courtyard with full-sized fifteenth-century French village houses and a Roman pool.

A diamond importer, Robert Schell, built a ninety-nine-room French-style castle in Northfield, Massachusetts, near the Vermont and New Hampshire borders as a wedding present for his bride. Today Schell Castle, which has since become an inn, is a favorite place for weddings.

Though he never married, the noted Shakespearean actor William Gillette entertained many beautiful women in his twenty-four room medieval Rhineland castle in Connecticut. Gillette Castle stands on the east bank of the Connecticut River on the heights above the Chester-Hadlyme Ferry between New Haven and New London.

Boldt Castle on thickly wooded Heart Island in the St. Lawrence River opposite Alexandria Bay, New York was begun by millionaire George C.

Boldt for his wife. Sadly, she did not live to see its completion. Upon her death, Boldt telegrammed the workmen to stop their saws and hammers. The castle fell quiet as a tomb as if Snow White was asleep and work would not progress until she awakened. But no fairy-tale miracle happened, and Boldt Castle remains empty and unfinished today.

Perhaps the most beautiful of America's castles, William Randolph Hearst's San Simeon, built against the Santa Lucia Mountains in California overlooking the ocean halfway between San Francisco and Los Angeles, was built in loving memory of his mother. He ordered the $35 million castle and grounds created as a shrine of beauty. Hearst lived there, his children grew up there, and the rich, famous, and royal came to visit and left in awe.

At least one of America's castles is haunted. Baranov's Castle was built in Sitka, Alaska, in the early 1800s by a wealthy Russian fur trader before Alaska became an American territory. Legend goes that a beautiful Russian princess was to marry a handsome, young cavalryman, but his superior officer, in jealousy, sent him on a mission that took his life. Later, on the night of her wedding to the officer, she disappeared from the ballroom in the midst of a gay bridal party. After a search of the castle, her body was found in one of the small drawing rooms. Those who lived in the castle afterward said her ghost haunted the halls.

Most of America's castles are now open to visitors for a few dollars admission. They stand as miracles of architecture, housing fabulous antiques and art treasures from all over the world. But what makes them most unique is the love stories that went into their creation.

Main Staircase
Biltmore House and Gardens

Mrs. Vanderbilt's Bedroom
Biltmore House and Gardens

My Love

My love for you is something rare,
Strong and vibrant like mountain air;
And yet it's like the valleys low,
Deep and quiet in winter snow.

My love for you is most divine,
Cathedral-tall like forest pine,
Dressed in ermine, pure and white,
Iridescent, crystal-bright.

My love for you is filled with grace,
Neatly woven like snowflakes' lace,
Gently falling upon the ground
Like silent magic, so profound.

My love for you is heaven blue
With winter's clouds passing through,
Filled with tears of ice and snow
That brings a joy you'll never know.

Gertrude Rudberg

Ermine
Wraps

Alice Leedy Mason

I have seen Winter, white and still,
Frosting up the distant hill.
At other times it hurries by
Tossing snow against the sky.

Most winter scenes that I have known
Cover space with white alone;
However, one I'd like to share
Remembers cardinals feeding there.

I have heard Winter in the night
Wailing like a banshee fight,
Churning drifts two feet and more,
Pounding on my cabin door.

Some winter sounds can be serene
When millponds enter in the scene.
Skating blades ring on the ice,
And vesper bells sound very nice.

I have seen beauty, tossed and curled,
Cover up a careworn world.
Ermine drapes the shabby woods
In lacy shawls and goose-down hoods.

Earth wears white for just one reason.
Snow and ice must come in season,
So man, at mountaintop, can see
The beauty of Eternity.

Blossom
Time

Though winter winds blow harsh and shrill,
I care not for their shrieking,
For apple blossoms grace a hill
That spring will soon be seeking.
Oh, lovely is my orchard fair
Where snow has fashioned flowers;
Bright April's presence lingers there
In white and shining bowers.
My world's a place of spring sublime
Because it's winter blossom time!

Brian F. King

Vistas
of Delight

Now winter with a lavish hand
Has scattered snow on country lanes
And garlanded with strings of pearls
A thousand frost-etched windowpanes.
Beneath the magic of her spell,
Where lovely landscapes lie serene,
Sweet-scented wisps of chimney smoke
Lend fragrance to the wondrous scene.
How bright the day! How dear the sight
Of sparkling vistas of delight!

Brian F. King

An Unfrozen Creek Bed

Sealing the last envelope of my son's valentines, I carefully gathered up leftover paste and sticky scissors. Proud of his childish accomplishments, he planned to mail homemade cards to each of his grandparents.

Project completed and two hours left before Mike would be home from his park ranger duties, we agreed upon a hike and zipped on our boots and nylon parkas. Warm breezes from the East Coast had begun to blow as we walked the Blue Ridge in the melting snow. We followed the wandering road, wistfully enjoying the last remains of a winter's snow.

With golden sunshine on our faces, we walked up the hill relishing the warmth this winter day. Laughing with childish nonsense, we played silly games like fox and geese in the softened snow. Spying a make-believe monster, Jamie raced excitedly over the hillside. It was exhilarating to be alive and to laugh with my son in the midst of God's sunshine.

Running on ahead, Jamie became tangled in the barbwire fence that bordered a meadow with a running stream. Pulling his jacket loose, I carefully lifted him over the fence and I crawled underneath to join him.

Sidestepping some frosty vegetation, my son and I stopped and beheld the winterized creek bed. Quickly its current raced past us, tumbling over rocks and stumps as it carried bits of ice. The snow with its crystal coat enhanced the beauty of the moving water.

This was a special time, a memorable time, I thought as I looked down at my giggling son. Throwing snowballs at the creek, we raced for a short distance. Thinking of the valentine he had set aside for me, I smiled with delight. Just having his love and my husband's was all I needed outside of God's love. I felt love from each one today.

Anxious to make a special supper for Mike, I took one last look at the enchanted landscape and started home. I lifted my son back over the wire fence, then he grabbed my hand and began to sing.

A prayer formed within me, inspired by the mood of the moment. Oh, Lord of creation, I thank You for love—for Your love and my family's—and the way it warms me inside. Thank You for the gifts You abundantly bestow on me: forgiveness of sin, caring and answering prayers, and sharing Yourself through nature. Somehow may I return Your love as I mature in mine. Allow me to be like the running current whose swirling waters always flow onward. Keep me moving daily as I travel toward a deeper faith. Never let me become cold, Father, stagnating or freezing in my relationships with You or my fellowman. Finally I ask You to continue to bless me, encourage me, chasten me, and teach me with Fatherly love so I may abound in faith, a flowing stream of Your love.

Diane Skinner

King of the winter,
   Robed in pure white,
Jeweled in crystal
   For children's delight;

Hat trimmed with cherries,
   Colors divine,
Temperature climbing
   Has forced his decline.

Under the sun
   He sinks to a huddle
To vanish at noonday,
   Only a puddle.

Myrtle George Latimer

Snow ❄ King

Valentine Tapestry

Special Thoughts About Valentines

We looked upon a world unknown,
On nothing we could call our own.
Around the glistening wonder bent
The blue walls of the firmament—
No cloud above, no earth below—
A universe of sky and snow!

John Greenleaf Whittier

Love, that geyser of the soul,
Can melt the ice and snow
Of the most frozen regions;
Wherever its warm springs well up,
There glows a southern climate.

Braden

Muse, bid the Morn awake!
Sad Winter now declines;
Each bird doth choose a mate;
This day's Saint Valentine's.
For that good bishop's sake
Get up and let us see
What beauty it shall be
That fortune us assigns.

Michael Drayton

Come live with me, and be my love,
And we will all the pleasures prove,
That valleys, groves, or hills, or fields,
Or woods and steepy mountains yield.

Christopher Marlowe

May God our hearts fore'er entwine—
I need you for my valentine!

George L. Ehrman

Love cannot be forced;
Love cannot be coaxed and teased.
It comes out of Heaven,
Unasked and unsought.

Pearl Buck

Love! Thy love pours down on mine
As the sunlight on the vine,
As the snow-rill on the vale,
As the salt breeze in the sail;
As the song unto the bird,
On my lips thy name is heard.

George Meredith

Oh, if it be to choose and call thee mine,
Love, thou art every day my Valentine!

Thomas Hood

To worship means never to dominate
Nor to hold half the heart in reserve;
For to love, truly love,
Means never to wish
To rule, but rather to serve.

Frank H. Keith

There is music
Even in the beauty
And the silent note
Which Cupid strikes,
Far sweeter than the sound
Of an instrument.

Sir Thomas Browne

Love is the light and sunshine of life.
We cannot fully enjoy ourselves or anything
unless someone we love
enjoys it with us.
Even if we are alone,
we store up our enjoyment
in hope of sharing it
hereafter with those we love.

Sir John Lubbock

A dab of paste has daubed the dart;
The ruffle is askew.
But its sweet message warms my heart—
DEAR MOTHER, I LOVE YOU.

Gail Brook Burket

So, little loveliest lady mine,
Here's my heart for your valentine!

Laura E. Richards

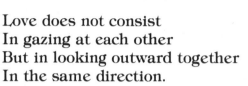

Cupid took aim—
Zing went the dart.
Every day is a valentine
With you in my heart!

Kay Hoffman

Love does not consist
In gazing at each other
But in looking outward together
In the same direction.

Antoine de Saint-Exupery

Compose a tender symphony;
gather robins, whippoorwills,
and larks;
but still the music
could not express
the love for you
within my heart.

Elizabeth St. Jacques

To love is to find pleasure
In the happiness of the person loved.

Leibnitz

Tomorrow is St. Valentine's Day,
All in the morning betime,
And I, a maid at your window,
To be your Valentine.

Shakespeare

The sea has its pearls,
The heaven its stars—
But my heart, my heart,
My heart has its love!

Heinrich Heine

CRYSTAL BEAUTY

The golden sun rose shining
Upon a world of ice,
And for that crystal beauty
Man could not pay the price.

The trees encased in silver
And some with golden hue
Stood etched in brilliant diamonds
Against the sky of blue.

The fields, the lawns, the meadows,
The hedge and fence tops, too,
Were all a frozen picture
Of what God's hand could do.

Gertrude Rudberg

JEWELED FRETWORK

This morning when I rose to look,
The world was like a storybook
With pictures of some far-off clime
Etched cunningly in silver rime.

The wire fence had ceased to be,
But in its place a tracery
Of jeweled fretwork climbed the sky
To where the radiant sun rolled by.

The birch, a diamond fountain bright
With rainbows, glowed with shimmering light;
Beneath the cedars' frosted lace
An opal rug was tucked in place.

Marjorie Freeman Campbell

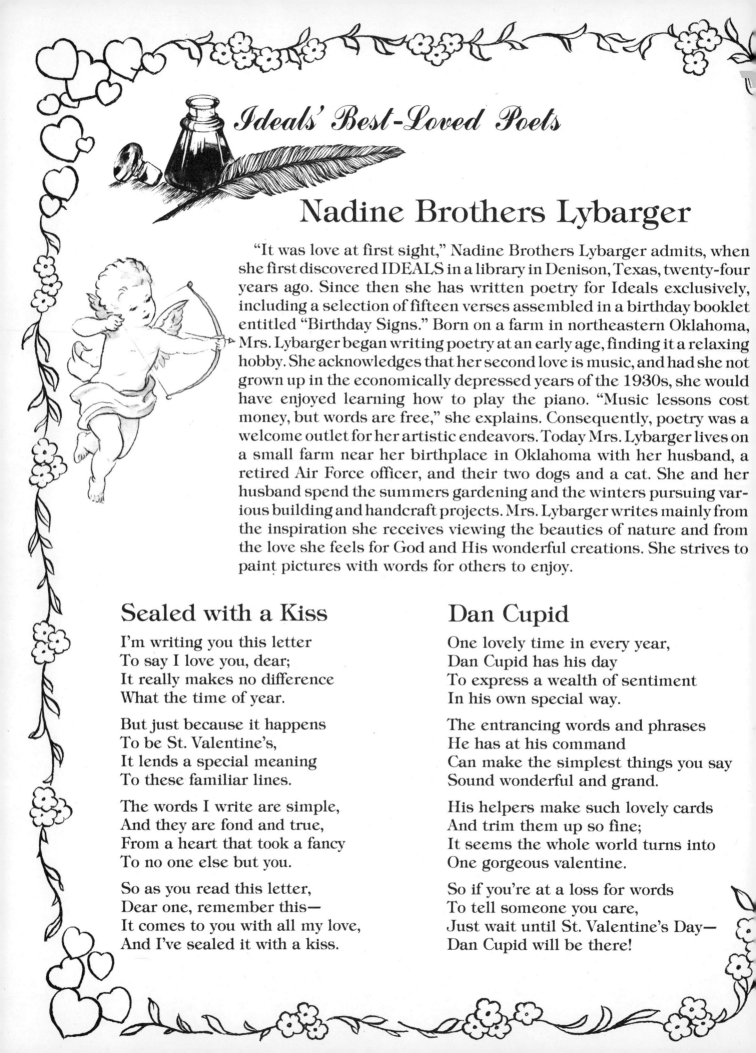

Nadine Brothers Lybarger

"It was love at first sight," Nadine Brothers Lybarger admits, when she first discovered IDEALS in a library in Denison, Texas, twenty-four years ago. Since then she has written poetry for Ideals exclusively, including a selection of fifteen verses assembled in a birthday booklet entitled "Birthday Signs." Born on a farm in northeastern Oklahoma, Mrs. Lybarger began writing poetry at an early age, finding it a relaxing hobby. She acknowledges that her second love is music, and had she not grown up in the economically depressed years of the 1930s, she would have enjoyed learning how to play the piano. "Music lessons cost money, but words are free," she explains. Consequently, poetry was a welcome outlet for her artistic endeavors. Today Mrs. Lybarger lives on a small farm near her birthplace in Oklahoma with her husband, a retired Air Force officer, and their two dogs and a cat. She and her husband spend the summers gardening and the winters pursuing various building and handcraft projects. Mrs. Lybarger writes mainly from the inspiration she receives viewing the beauties of nature and from the love she feels for God and His wonderful creations. She strives to paint pictures with words for others to enjoy.

Sealed with a Kiss

I'm writing you this letter
To say I love you, dear;
It really makes no difference
What the time of year.

But just because it happens
To be St. Valentine's,
It lends a special meaning
To these familiar lines.

The words I write are simple,
And they are fond and true,
From a heart that took a fancy
To no one else but you.

So as you read this letter,
Dear one, remember this—
It comes to you with all my love,
And I've sealed it with a kiss.

Dan Cupid

One lovely time in every year,
Dan Cupid has his day
To express a wealth of sentiment
In his own special way.

The entrancing words and phrases
He has at his command
Can make the simplest things you say
Sound wonderful and grand.

His helpers make such lovely cards
And trim them up so fine;
It seems the whole world turns into
One gorgeous valentine.

So if you're at a loss for words
To tell someone you care,
Just wait until St. Valentine's Day—
Dan Cupid will be there!

An Ever, Ever Valentine

Initials carved upon a tree—
What memories they recall,
For once love came a-courting me,
So handsome, straight, and tall.

Hand in hand we strolled, and I
Blushed to hear him whisper, "True,
Cross my heart and hope to die,
Always, dearest, I'll love you."

Then he carved upon "our" tree
A heart for all the world to see
With his initials pledged to mine,
An ever, ever valentine.

What shy, young lover has not known
The thrill of being one's alone—
First tender kiss, first tender sigh,
And Cupid's shadow passing by?

Now there is silver in the gold;
My love and I are growing old;
With something borrowed, something blue,
I saw my childhood dream come true.

And as we shared throughout the years
All our happiness and tears,
His heart became entwined with mine—
An ever, ever valentine.

If I Could Choose

If I could choose
A valentine
For you to send
To me,
I wouldn't care about
Its size
Or how it looked,
You see.

I wouldn't care if
Words it held
Were numerous or few,
Just so they said in
Substance, dear,
"I give my heart to you."

Though love would give,
Not take, they say,
My heart would surely pine
Unless you give your
Love to me
And be my valentine.

A Valentine Message

What I would say to you, my love,
Has been said many times—
Fond words of praise in whispered phrase
And sweetly worded rhymes.

Although I know no new approach,
I'd like to make it clear,
The thoughts I hold are special ones
For you alone, my dear.

And if my message isn't new,
I'm sure that you will know
It's different 'cause it's just for you—
Dear one, I love you so!

Hand in Hand

If I may walk with you, my love,
My feet shall never go astray;
This age-old promise ever new
I give you with my heart today.

No trial, then, too great to bear,
No challenge that I dare not meet,
As long as you are there to care,
I find my pathways all are sweet.

You are my key to happiness
In everything I strive to do.
I ask of life no more than this—
To walk, love, hand in hand with you.

Midst frills and hearts and dainty lace,
　I take a noble stand
Because I will employ them all
　To win your lovely hand.

I'll tell you of my earnest love
　And what you mean to me,
As if by now you didn't know,
　As if you couldn't see!

I'll wish you, dearest Valentine,
　A very happy day
With everything most wonderful
　Coming all your way.

I love you, dear, and I can see
　Love mirrored in your face;
I take a noble stand amidst
　The hearts and bits of lace!

Georgia B. Adams

Midst
Frills and
Hearts

Dear Valentine

Dear Valentine, I send my love
Within these words I write;
I send devotion, tender thoughts,
And moments of delight,
Expressing all the warmth and joy,
Each loving sweet caress,
With hopes and dreams that you shall find
Along with happiness.

Dear Valentine, I send my heart,
Affection, dear and true,
Because this heart that is my own
Belongs to only you.
I cannot tell in words alone
Just all you mean to me,
And yet I send my fondest thoughts
That surely you shall see.

Love finds a way to touch a heart,
To set a world aglow;
'Tis ever bright and beautiful;
I feel that you must know
How very special you've become
Within this life of mine.
Once more today I send my love
To you—dear Valentine.

Garnett Ann Schultz

White World

All around the house tonight,
All around the town,
Feathery flakes of crystal snow
Are drifting gently down.

They dim the shape of tree and shrub
And pad the walk with white
And make each streetlamp's golden rays
Look soft as candlelight.

They settle on the windowsill,
Creep upward as we stare
In fascination at this wealth
Of whiteness everywhere.

Oh, surely even fairyland
With all its magic glow
Could not be lovelier than this
White world of winter snow!

Virginia Blanck Moore

John Svobodnik

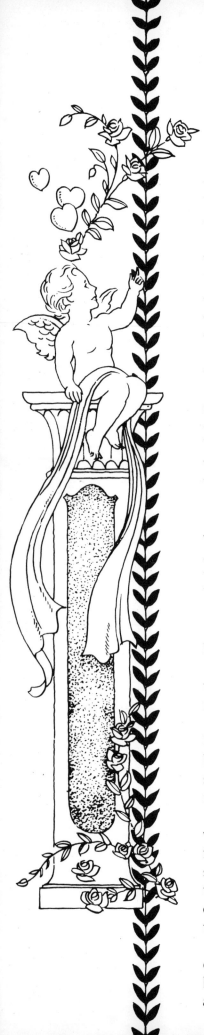

Valentine's Day Is a Heart-Shaped Holiday

Martha Tarpley Baker

Hearts adorned with birds, lace, flowers, and cupids symbolize the sentimental, but lighthearted holiday on the fourteenth of February. Known as Saint Valentine's Day, the event itself might have vanished, but the strange turnabout of its symbol kept it alive.

The oldest known valentine was sent by Charles, Duke of Orleans, to his wife while he was imprisoned in 1415 in the Tower of London. In his famous diary, Samuel Pepys describes a valentine received by his wife, and later he grumbles about the high cost of valentine tokens expected by the ladies from their admirers, listing such items as gloves, shoestrings, silk stockings, fancy garters, and jewelry in his complaint!

No one is really sure who Saint Valentine was. The early church lists a number of martyrs by this name, and the Feast Day for all of them is the fourteenth of February. The legends surrounding them are as numerous as the martyrs themselves. One version is that Emperor Claudius II, during the third century A.D., decreed that no soldier could marry or become engaged. A Roman priest named Valentine was convinced that married soldiers would not be anxious to start wars, and so he married many of the young couples in secret. Upon discovery he was seized and put to death on the fourteenth of February.

Another legend contends that a Roman named Valentine was thrown into prison for aiding the persecuted Christians. While in jail this Valentine converted to Christianity, became a friend of the jailer's blind daughter, and through a miracle restored her sight. On the morning of his execution, again the fourteenth of February, he sent the young girl a message signed "From your Valentine."

Whatever may be the truth concerning Saint Valentine himself, it is known that February fourteenth was the eve of an important Roman festival long before the birth of Christ and the advent of the Christian martyrs. The festival day was called Lupercalia, and since February was a spring month in the old Roman calendar, the celebration most likely had to do with spring crops and fertility. Records mark Lupercalia being observed as early as 445 B.C.

By the time of Julius Caesar, however, the original reason for the holiday had long been forgotten, and Lupercalia was a day of frolic and feasting highlighted by each young man drawing from a decorated urn the name of his so-called sweetheart or partner for the festivities. Often these young men pinned the girl's name to the arm of their garment, thus truly "wearing their heart on their sleeve."

With the establishment of the Roman church throughout Europe, an attempt was made to eliminate the pagan observances by converting them to Christian feast days. Thus Saint Valentine's Day was created, and an attempt was made to substitute the drawing of a saint's name in lieu of a young girl partner. Needless to say, this was not greeted with much enthusiasm. Pairing of young couples continued throughout Europe, often with such raucous results that it was eventually banned in many countries including France and Italy.

England and, in turn, the American colonies in the New World continued to observe Valentine's Day as a sweetheart's day. Heart-shaped valentines were handmade and hand-delivered to the chosen young woman, sometimes accompanied by a tiny pair of paper gloves or a pair of real gloves. Gloves symbolized asking for "a woman's hand in marriage," and if the young lady chose to wear the gloves at the following Easter service, she indicated her acceptance of the proposal!

The heart still dominated all valentines, but other symbols also were used. Love knots were gracefully looped paper or silk ribbons with no beginning or end, imprinted with messages of love. A favorite of the ladies was to give a watch paper to their sweethearts. These hand-painted papers or embroidered silk circles replaced the ordinary paper used to keep dust out of a man's pocketwatch.

The earliest machine-made valentines were postcards (it was twice as costly to send an enclosed message) and were usually woodcuts or lithographs. By 1840, with envelopes in common use, valentines became more elegant and exceedingly elaborate.

Although valentines were usually sent to sweethearts, close friends, and family members, occasionally they were mail-delivered to a person the sender greatly disliked! These "vinegar valentines" were spiteful and, obviously, usually unsigned. Despite their antipathy to the usual sentiments of the day, these lampooning valentines were masterpieces of the comic and grotesque.

Until the mid-nineteenth century, most of the valentines exchanged in the United States were imported from Germany and England. In 1848, a Miss Esther Howard, daughter of a Massachusetts stationer, admired some of the fancy English valentines in her father's shop and decided to try her hand at making her own. So popular were the resulting lacy reproductions that Esther soon found herself obliged to ask her friends to help fill the orders, and she set up an assembly-line process for making the cards.

For many years Miss Howard was the prime maker of valentines in this country and was noted both for her innovative production methods as well as being one of the first American women to own her own business. Esther Howard did much to increase the popularity of exchanging valentines in the United States and is credited with introducing the lovely three-dimensional, stand-up greeting card. During the Civil War, special valentines were created for the soldiers and their sweethearts. Called "window-designs," they featured tent flaps or church windows that opened to reveal a lone soldier or a soldier and his bride inside.

The Victorian age was truly the golden age of the valentine with silk, satin, real lace, tiny mirrors, and locks of hair incorporated into the designs. A blank space was left for the sender to inscribe his own verse, and the result was that many Victorian cards were far more elegant than their enclosed sentiment. So-called "Valentine Writers," booklets of verse for all occasions, were highly popular.

Valentines have a tendency to follow the trend of the times, and by 1880, the cards were increasingly gaudy with fringes, tassels, feathers, and beads. Probably due to their tackiness, adult valentines were passé by the 1920s, and Valentine's Day was almost exclusively a children's holiday. Grade-schoolers throughout the country eagerly anticipated the opening of the large red and white, heart-trimmed valentine box placed in each classroom for the fourteenth of February, and "how many did you get?" was a frequent question.

Not until World War II did valentines regain importance in the adult world. This was caused by a popular demand from soldiers overseas wishing to send greetings to their sweethearts and family back home.

Today, valentines are no longer just for sweethearts and family. They are sent to friends, relatives, neighbor children, prospective "dates," and would-be customers. The valentine has almost become a friendship card, while expressions of love now come under the guise of a box of candy, a silver locket, a red picture frame, or a dozen roses. Still, the ancient traditional symbol remains intact—on Valentine's Day, love comes in the shape of a heart!

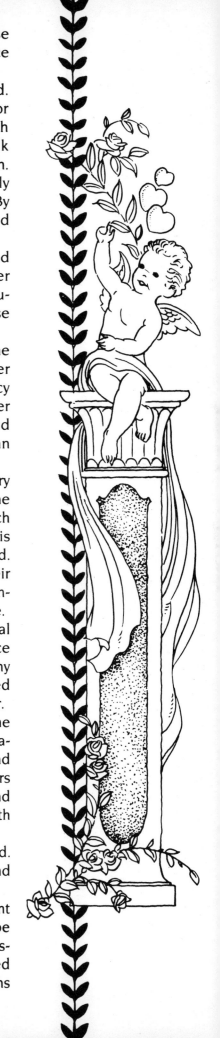

Valentine Treats

St. Valentine's—the day of sweets
Inspires from the kitchen, fragrant treats.
A banquet of love from the heart is shared
When special dishes are prepared.

The cook has captured every heart
In setting this gladsome day apart.
Fulfilling many a savory wish,
Her love has seasoned every dish.

Linda Robinson

The wind moaned over the open field rattling the frozen grass that extended above the snow-covered ground. On this icy February day, no living being could be sighted except two cold hikers searching for some of nature's winter creatures. A few deer tracks were found along the bluff, but not a single bird or mammal had stirred. Suddenly, a flock of white- and brown-colored sparrows flitted into the air, whirled about in unison cheerfully twittering, and alighted again to continue their feeding. These were seldom seen snowbirds that had temporarily come south from the Arctic to enjoy the warmer weather. Like sunbathers on a warm spring day, they were basking in the milder temperatures which were fifty to seventy-five degrees warmer than their home territory. (When the weather moderates further north, they return to their favorite northern feeding and nesting sites for the remainder of the year.)

Birds are the most common fall and winter migrants, but a few mammals also avoid severe winter conditions by territorial movement. Evidence of the migratory urge is also seen in man.

Although people enjoy the changing seasons, most northern dwellers wish the winter season was at least one or two months shorter. This is particularly true of senior citizens. They have more difficulty enduring the extreme indoor/outdoor temperature fluctuations and are much more subject to the cold and flu viruses that abound in the colder months. Ice and snow cover makes walking and driving more treacherous and limits outdoor activities. Being housebound for weeks can cause nervous irritability called "cabin fever." The yearning for sunshine, milder temperatures, and more pleasant outdoor living has created a migration that has been further stimulated by the lower cost of living in southern areas.

Of those who permanently move to warmer climates, less than twenty percent are over the age of fifty-five. The more mature adults often prefer their familiar surroundings and close proximity to family and friends. Instead of relocating in a new area, many avoid the long winter season by moving south for part or all of the cold period, returning as the weather improves. These are the "snowbirds," the human migrators of the North. The migration is given further

impetus by the heat and/or humidity that develops in many southern areas in the summer season.

Is it wise to become a snowbird? Millions of retired people think so. However, there are certain disadvantages that should be considered. If a person wishes to maintain a permanent northern home, most of its expenses continue whether it is occupied or not. Some people avoid these costs to a degree by living in a trailer on a part-time or full-time basis. Others have developed lease agreements at both ends of the migration, a difficult task in many areas. Since inflation has increased the cost of housing, automobiles and food, the cost of travel should be carefully considered.

To leave family, friends and familiar surroundings for a short time is not too difficult, provided a pleasant living pattern can be established at the new site. Snowbirds can accomplish this more easily if they locate among other snowbirds or in a friendly community happy to accept and accommodate them. Migrating adults should consider their desired church associations, medical needs, social activities, and recreational opportunities. Their living sites should provide these needs. If tempted to take up permanent residence in the warmer climate they should test the situation for at least a year before making any radical changes. Particularly, they should live in the new area during the less comfortable time of the year to experience the full range of conditions.

Too many senior citizens needlessly feel unwanted or of little importance in our society after retirement. These feelings can be exaggerated when people move into strange territories. The most contented and happiest people are often those who find ways of contributing to the community in which they are living. When directing some of their talents, skills, and efforts into charitable activities they soon realize that they are not only wanted but are greatly needed. The knowledge, wisdom and understanding of mature people are valuable commodities in a confused and frail world.

By giving of their long years of experience, these people receive a great deal in return, not the least of which is a feeling of self-esteem and contentment. The snowbirds should be valuable members of the communities at both ends of their migration.

Harold W. Rock

The Flower of the Heart

A flower from thee is blooming
    Upon the table there.
Its lovely fragrance wafts to me
    Upon the silent air.

And though it's lovely to my eyes,
    It never can compare
To that which blooms within my heart,
    Thy friendship true and fair.

True friendship is a jewel rare,
    A treasure from above;
Two hearts may hold it just one way
    In mutual trust and love.

Maramel Lemara

Treasures

What special gifts would I bring to thee
To prove my love's sincerity?

A sunlit day to warm your soul
And drive life's hurts away,

A corner of a woods I know
Where a stream runs clear and bluebells grow,

A warbling song which ebbs and flows
From a small bluebird with breast of rose,

Misted mountain peaks adrift in snow
Where the golden sunrise sets a fire aglow,

A mountain meadow from pattern divine
Embroidered by God from blue columbine,

My old apple tree with its oriole nest,
A hidden lake where the osprey rests,

The mirror-surfaced ocean where setting sun
Reflects its radiance as evening comes,

These my treasures would I give to thee
To prove my love's sincerity.

Norma Fore

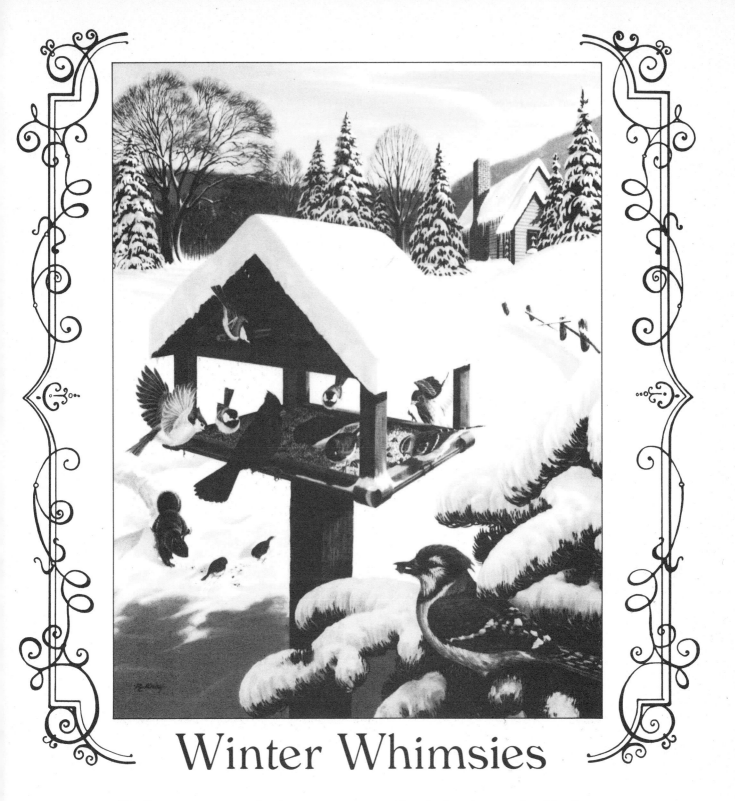

Winter Whimsies

Birdhouse snow confections
Like Christmas gingercake,
Opalescent ice-drops
Winter's jewelry make.
Fence posts decked in clown hats,
Pinecones, poufs of snow,
And snowmen small,
And snowmen tall,
Everywhere I go.

My window box a glacé loaf,
The marsh wears tinseled reeds,
And flung across
The stark white lawn,
Cat-print strings of beads.
And though the blustering north wind
Flails with icy sting,
Winter whimsies make me smile
While I wait for spring.

Violet Bigelow Rourke

Twelve Roses

Twelve roses here for you:
The first one brings my love;
The second says that you
Are the one I'm dreaming of;

The third red rose is gladness—
So may it bring to you;
The fourth is our first kiss,
But what can kisses do?

The fifth red rose is tears—
We both have shed a few;
The sixth rose is the times
We've shared, both old and new;

The seventh is the day
We met not long ago;
The eighth is you and me
And the happiness we'd know;

The ninth red rose is for
The hand I've often held;
The tenth rose is much more—
It's the love that we could build;

The eleventh is the fun
We've had so many times;
The twelfth rose is the one
That carries but a line—
The important rose is this one,
For this one says, "Be mine."

J. Michael Pawlusiak

So Is Love

Frances McKinnon Morton

Rose of the hearthfire,
White of the snow,
Strength of the steel
In the furnace glow,
Tender as infancy,
Fragrant as flowers,
Warm as the sunshine,
Fruitful as showers—
So is love in a life.

The Sweetest Flower

Frederick Peterson

The sweetest flower that blows
I give you as we part;
For you it is a rose;
For me it is my heart.

The fragrance it exhales—
Ah, if you only knew—
Which but in dying fails,
It is my love for you.

The sweetest flower that blows
I give you as we part;
You think it but a rose;
Ah me, it is my heart.

How Could He Throw Me Over Like That?

Well, that does it! Harold has rejected me. I was faithful for months and what did I get? Jilted!

Of course, it isn't the first time. I've been rejected by spider plants before, you know. In fact, I'm a veteran of several wars—the White Fly Invasion, the Mealy-bug Melee, and the Root-rot Conflict.

Ah, yes, the Root-rot Conflict. Now there was a nasty one. All those casualties, you know. Not just spider plants, but begonias, African violets, philodendron, and even a peperomia or two. You hand me a plant, any plant, and I can rot its roots. That takes talent. It also runs up my water bill.

Somehow Harold's defection seemed more personal, though. You see, he not only turned against me, but he turned thumbs down on my whole lifestyle. I'd have understood if he had just curled up and died. It's happened before.

But not Harold. He languished. He turned yellow, lost leaves, didn't grow. He looked pitiful; he was limp. Finally he attracted the attention of my teenage son, who volunteered to adopt Harold and provide him with a home for his last days. He tenderly hung Harold in a bright macrame hanger in his bedroom window.

"Ha!" I said to myself. "A week in that den of disaster and he'll be glad enough to crawl back into the study and grow like a civilized plant should."

Instead—and this is the part that hurts—Harold has found a new life. He stands up straight and proud, ruling the window with authority. He puts out new leaves—green ones even. In short, I've been jilted.

"What did you do?" I asked my son.

"Harold likes it here," he said. "It's a more interesting atmosphere."

"You're right," I agreed. "Dirty socks are very stimulating."

"Besides, I talk to him," he added.

"What do you find to talk about?" I asked.

"Well," he admitted sheepishly, "I did teach him some bad words, but he only uses them when I forget to open the curtains before I go to school."

So there you have it. For all I know, the kid may be watering him with root beer.

Whatever it is, Harold is a new plant. I've been trying hard to learn the system, but it doesn't come easily. I guess there must be a knack to it.

In desperation I attempted to say a bad word to an ivy. The shock killed it. I left a half-eaten sandwich under a Chinese evergreen for a week, but all I got was ants.

You see? Everywhere I turn—rejection. Finally I swallowed my pride and knocked on my son's door, potted plant in hand.

"Would you see what you can do with this jade plant?" I asked. "It seems to be sick."

"What's its name?"

"Jade."

"Hmmm. Not very imaginative, but I'll do my best," he said.

This time I've got him. I've known that jade for a long time. It's a terrible hypochondriac.

Nona Morrison

The fence posts wear white caps of snow though winter's
Ebbing now, and calendars insist
Now is the time for spring to make a show.
Eaves and limbs still glitter with bright splinters
Of crystal ice; small winter birds still tryst
With icicles along the cedar row;
But there is green within each tube of ice,
And under the river's opalescent shell,
A trickle murmurs with a sound of spring.

I have loved winter, but I don't think twice
When asked if I am ready for the swell
Of sap and northbound flight of absent wing.
I shall watch daily as the fence posts lengthen
And grassroots nibble through the snow at last;
I shall get out for longer spells each day.
And as these lands beneath the pale sun strengthen,
And long, housed nights seem pleasanter, once past,
I know I love spring more—in a conservative way.

Edsel Ford

Spring Song, with Reservations

Sap's Running

Sap's running in the maple trees;
The smell of earth is in the air.
Although the wind is raw and cold,
The feel of spring is everywhere.
This morning ere the sun came up,
I saw a robin zooming down,
A hardy pioneer, no doubt,
Looking up housing in the town.

The maple bush is all alive
With light and shade and pitted snow.
Blue smoke is drifting through the trees;
Above a hill I heard a crow
Giving a broadcast of events
To fellow crows, who listened in
From the split rail atop the fence.

On every maple tree there hangs
A wooden pail to catch the sap,
As drop by drop it slowly falls
From the small nozzle of the tap.
In the pale liquid, clear as wine,
A few small twigs and leaves have blown,
Combining with the frost and sun
To give a flavor of their own.

A dozen children gather round
The steaming kettle's fragrant glow,
Begging their dad to pour the sap
Into their little pans of snow.
Earth holds no greater joy, I swear,
No sweeter charm can heaven bring,
Than maple trees warmed by the sun
Where sap is running in the spring.

Edna Jaques

February

The waiting time—a quiet world
When snow is all about,
No grass of green, no singing birds,
No warmth without a doubt,
It surely is the time between
With winter dreams to share,
A frosty morn, an evening cool,
And snowflakes everywhere.

February sometimes lends
A touch of springtime charms,
A bit of magic, gentle winds
To catch with outstretched arms,
A different kind of winter world
With oft a bit of sun,
As patiently we watch and wait
For special winter fun.

A time between—and yet so dear,
Bright hopes of fall just past
While looking forward to the spring
Amidst the winter's blast,
For February is a span;
It tells of things to be,
A bridge connecting fall and spring
We travel happily.

Garnett Ann Schultz

This winter day is fringed with hush and frost,
And snowflakes eddy down the crystal stair;
So carelessly released and lightly tossed,
They drift to earth and settle everywhere.
Familiar places I have come to know
Have strangely vanished quickly into space,
Half-hidden by a wall of driven snow,
And look quite foreign in their mask of lace.

Transition

A little while and then I will reclaim
Familiar places, edged with beads of gold,
And sight an orchard in a pool of flame,
Forgetful of the stinging sleet and cold.
And soon the birds will fill our hearts with song,
Pouring their liquid sweetness all day long.

Charlotte Abetz

A Gift

What gift would I bring, if I could,
To say "I love you so"?
I'd like to give a thousand days,
Tied with a velvet bow,

Not crimson days of skyrockets
And thrilling memories,
But quiet times of love and peace
To do with as you please,

With hours for friends, and love that stays
Without need to be won,
Moments of solitude and thought,
But also time for fun.

I'd like you to be able to
Enjoy each simple thing:
How roadside snowbanks suddenly
Run melting into spring;

How summer winds shake out the dusk
When each long day is done;
Or how a golden maple glows,
So radiant in the sun.

I want you to have time to see
Snow-fingers brushing trees
And flowers in a rain-swept field
That laugh up to the breeze.

We all have felt great days of joy
And aching sadness, too,
But we weave life of simple days—
That's what I wish for you.

Heather Kirkwood

COLOR ART AND PHOTO CREDITS
(in order of appearance)

Front and back cover, Gerald Koser; inside front cover, Gerald Koser; Winter berries, Fred Sieb; Scenic drive near Hadlyme, Connecticut, Freelance Photographers Guild; Gift of carnations, Robert Cushman Hayes; Fleurette figurine, Cybis Porcelains; Valentine message, Fred Sieb; Little sweetheart, Freelance Photographers Guild; Valentine treats, Tom Stack; Old-fashioned valentines from the collection of Evelyn and Lester Dallmann, Gerald Koser; Flowers and candy, Gerald Koser; Little Cottonwood Canyon near Mt. Superior in the Wasatch Mountains, Utah, Josef Muench; Cross-country skiers, Freelance Photographers Guild; Farm near Stafford Hollow, Connecticut, Alpha Photo Associates; Snow king, Colour Library International (USA) Limited; Winter draperies, Josef Muench; Figurines and flowers, Fred Sieb; COZY DWELLING, John Slobodnik; Fragrant kitchen, Colour Library International (USA) Limited; The key to my heart, Gerald Koser; Snow-covered birdhouse, Fred Sieb; Gift of roses, Robert Cushman Hayes; Pink rose, Fred Sieb; Dana River in California, Colour Library International (USA) Limited; Coverlet of beauty, Robert Holland; Sap pails near Conway, New Hampshire, Fred Sieb; A gift of love, Gerald Koser; inside back cover, Gerald Koser.

Statement of ownership, management and circulation (Required by 39 U.S.C., 3685), of IDEALS, published 8 times a year in: Feb.; Mar.; Apr.; June; Aug.; Sept.; Nov.; Dec. at Milwaukee, Wisconsin for September 1981. Publisher, Ideals Publishing Corporation; Editor, James A. Kuse; Managing Editor, Ralph Luedtke; Owner, Harlequin Holdings, Inc., 306 South State Street, Dover, Delaware 19901. The known bondholders, mortgagees, and other security holders owning or holding 1 percent or more of total amount of bonds, mortgages or other securities are: None. Average no. copies each issue during preceding 12 months: Total no. copies printed (Net Press Run) 318,074. Paid circulation 82,217. Mail subscriptions 160,751. Total paid circulation 242,968. Free distribution 741. Total distribution 243,709. Single issue published nearest to filing date: Total no. copies printed (Net Press Run) 196,856. Paid circulation 9,247. Other sales 155,124. Free distribution 379. Total distribution 164,750. I certify that the statements made by me are correct and complete. Donald A. Gottschalk, President.

ACKNOWLEDGMENTS

BECAUSE OF YOU by Eunice Elmore Heizer. From ECHOES by Eunice Elmore Heizer, Copyright © 1967 by Eunice Elmore Heizer. Published by Dorrance & Company. ST. VALENTINE'S DAY by Essie L. Mariner. From her book ENCOUNTERED. A DAY OF SWEETNESS by W. R. Morrison. From THE HAWK AND THE BUTTERFLY by W. R. Morrison, Copyright © 1977 by W. R. Morrison. Published by Dorrance & Company. SO IS LOVE by Frances McKinnon Morton. From her book I SAW THE MORNING STAR, Copyright © 1938 by Henry Harrison. Used with permission of Ward M. Morton. A DAY OF LOVE (originally titled: ST. VALENTINE'S DAY) by Letitia Morse Nash. From SINGING WORDS by Letitia Morse Nash, Copyright © 1949 by Letitia Morse Nash. TWELVE ROSES by J. Michael Pawlusiak. From A ROSE IS ... by J. Michael Pawlusiak, Copyright © 1970 by Michael Pawlusiak. Published by Dorrance & Company. LOOKING FOR SPRING (originally titled: GROUNDHOG DAY) by Marnie Pomeroy. Reprinted with permission of the author. VALENTINE'S DAY by Margaret Rorke. From her book AN OLD CRACKED CUP, Copyright © 1980 by Northwood Institute Press. Used with permission. Our sincere thanks to the following authors whose addresses we were unable to locate: Edsel Ford for SPRING SONG, WITH RESERVATIONS; Anne M. Robinson for BARBERRY RED.

Join us in celebrating Easter and springtime!

Easter Ideals presents a vivid portrayal of spring and all its glories: colorful tulips and daffodils in bloom, trees green with new buds, and woodland creatures frolicking in the sunshine. Interesting articles, prose, and poetry accompany the beautiful color photographs and artwork.

Make the Spring season special for family and friends by giving a gift subscription to Ideals, beginning with our Easter issue. A world of beauty will be yours to enjoy year round!